To Ursula

Our Wonderful Fragile Life

J.G. Clarke

Best Wishes

George

19 Apr '25

Dedication

To my late, wonderful wife Eileen M.

The Robin featured above is in memory of my late wife. Many years ago, a cheeky little Robin, built her nest in our greenhouse and stayed several years. Every morning, the Robin came to the kitchen window and gave it a tap and my wife would hold out a nut or another titbit. The Robin would land on her hand for its breakfast without any fear, as did one of its off-spring years later.

This quote is a favourite of my late wife's, which still hangs on my kitchen wall:

> *"I expect to pass through this world but once.*
> *Any good thing, therefore, that I can do,*
> *or any kindness that I can show to any fellow being,*
> *let me do it now.*
> *Let me not defer or neglect it,*
> *for I shall not pass this way again."*

Stephen Grellet,[1] *1772-1855.*

---

[1] A prominent French-American missionary, whose father was a counsellor of King Louis XV1.

OUR WONDERFUL FRAGILE LIFE

Copyright © 2025 by J.G. Clarke

ISBN 978-1-915223-43-2

All rights reserved.

No part of this publication may be reproduced, stored in a retrieval system, or transmitted in any form or by any means, electronic, mechanical, photocopying or otherwise, without prior written consent of the publisher except as provided by under United Kingdom copyright law. Short extracts may be used for review purposes with credits given.

Published by

Maurice Wylie Media
Your Inspirational & Christian Book Publisher

For more information visit
www.MauriceWylieMedia.com

Contents

Introduction 13
Time 15
A Farmer's Son 17
Adversity 19
The Soul 20
Never Rush Trouble 21
The Start 22
Enlightenment 23
Dreams 25
Cruelty of Man 26
Mind Games 27
Church Mouse 28
Work 29
Earth Warming 30
Love nor Money 31
Day to Day Living 32
Portrush 33
The Train 34
The Final Call 35
Modern Warfare 36

The Dawn Chorus	37
A Penny for your Thoughts	39
Cereal	40
Children	41
Awareness	43
Marriage	44
The Model	45
Signs of Age	46
Nightmares	48
Let Not a Tear Drop Fall	49
Christmas Dinner	50
The Theatre of Dreams	51
The Passing Wind	52
Lonely Ben	53
Sweet Life	54
The Purpose of Life	55
Good or Bad	56
Happiness	57
Granny's Whistle	59
Experience	60
Return of Summer	61
Hell's Gate	62
The Proposal	63
Love	64
Hope Springs	65

Politics	66
The Blackbird	67
Life and Death	68
Precious Moments	69
Living	70
Dubai	71
A Promise	72
Late Autumn	73
The Bus Pass	75
The Mobile Phone	76
Lucky	77
Choice	78
Broadhaven Bay	79
War Memories	80
War	82
The Weather	83
Belief	84
Chance	85
Life	86
Ignorance	87
Secrets	88
School Days	89
Life and Strife	91
Hands-free Doctors	92
Bags of Happiness and Laughter	93

Absence	94
Wishes	95
What Others See	96
The Robin	97
Early Winter	98
The Upspoken Word	99
Hope	100
The Rush	101
Innocence	102
The Huntsman	103
No	104
The Red Squirrel	105
Gift or Talent	106
Scotia	107
The Wrong Man	109
The Grim Reaper	110
The Lady on the Beach	111
The Bishop's Dream	112
Word Play	113
Borrowing	114
Rock of Cashel	115
Sand Erosion at Strandhill	116
Talk	117
Future	118

Introduction

We often hear Academics and Scholars interpreting famous poems by famous poets, telling us what the poet "really" meant. But Clarke's poems require no such analysis. He writes about life exactly as he sees it—honest, refreshing, and, at times, amusing, and in plain language to suit all ages. He comments, "If the reader can find at least one poem, which causes them to sit up and look again at this wonderful life, then I shall be happy."

The first and last poems in the book, "***Time***" and "***Future***" are sure to put us all in a reflective mood.

Time

As we travel slowly daily,
on our journey through this life,
The clock it keeps on ticking,
through happiness or strife.
Father Time is our enemy,
make no mistake when you hear his feet.
He won't stop for anyone,
as he marches to his constant beat.
If you watch an hourglass,
you can see time pass.
Or hear it tick on a clock,
it journeys on relentlessly,
as steady as a rock.
"I need more time"
is a cry we often hear each day.
The wish is never granted,
at work or during play.
We all have a finite portion of time,
as we live this life.
We all have a limited time,
to love a husband or wife.
A limited time to play a game,
to catch a bus or even a plane.
Some use time wisely,
some don't really care.

Some treat it with contempt,
and some would never dare.
As we reach the end of life,
we see it can't be bought.
Good times or bad times,
they all come to nought.
No matter what the price we pay,
we cannot buy another day.
Father Time is omnipotent,
he never takes a seat.
He's always there, he never leaves,
ever nodding to his beat.
You can't retrieve time, once its past,
the clock keeps ticking, the die is cast.
Enjoy your time, with all your might,
When it's finally up,
you'll not have one more night.
You won't hear the clock stop, have no doubt,
when your time allowed, has finally run out.

A Farmer's Son

There is no future in farming,
no money to be made.
Never a fortune will be earned,
by using a fork or a spade.

"Choose another way of life",
said the farmer to his son, one day.
Journey to the city,
and find another way.

He did as his father suggested,
and found a job learning a Trade.
At Harland and Wolf in the city,
where very large ships were made.

He started work on one of these ships,
and worked on her for years.
And when the work was finished,
she was launched to many cheers.

He was chosen by Harland and Wolff
to sail on her very first trip,
but his newly wedded wife said "No",
and he had to bite his lip.

Titanic set off on her journey,
destination U.S.A,
but she never reached her Harbour,
an Iceberg got in her way.

When the Farmer's son heard the news,
he ran to tell his wife.
They cried for all the poor souls lost,
and were thankful he still had his life.

Adversity

Adversity is so well armed,
and very hard to face.
It has a way of creeping back,
just when we thought we'd won the race.
And though we stand 'mid trouble and strife,
we try to carry on with life.
Each day its many troubles bring,
At night we dream the same,
and as the dawn breaks in the sky,
we start the cycle off again.
Peace 'O peace where art thou,
can you not heed cries of pain.
Must we face adversity,
Again and again and again.

The Soul

What thoughts shall I have in my conscious mind,
when the final bell rings out.
Is it time to worry about my Soul,
has its path been carved through doubt.
Who will I meet on this final march,
Others will have heard the bell.
Will the route be upwards,
or downwards to the Gates of Hell.
Did the weight of being good,
outweigh my times of being bad.
Did my daily outlook on life,
now cause to make me sad.
Life will present a bill to pay,
this cannot be changed come what may.
It was never a fear, and never a goal,
to know the resting place of my Soul.

Never Rush Trouble

Let things cool said the wise old fool,
never rush into trouble.
Take your time, play it cool,
and make sure your troubles don't double.
But I can't let things develop,
I need to fix it without delay.
Not so, not so, just take your time,
bad trouble seldom keeps at bay.
Sleep on your problems,
and they may go away,
things look vastly different,
in the cool light of day.

The Start

There is a sound we cannot hear,
a sound from far away.
Sent from different Galaxies,
each and every day.

These sound waves have been travelling,
for Billions of years and more.
Shaking our reasoning of the Universe, and Life,
to its very centre core.

How and why, and where and when,
are we ever destined to know.
Did things really start with a bang,
a long, long time ago?

Enlightenment

Holy men and Scholars,
with riches they are not content.
They seek what's very hard to find
they seek Enlightenment.
This is their only goal in life,
it brings such peace of mind.
The reason for the Universe,
the existence of Mankind.

When the blackboard of the mind is cleaned,
will the way ahead be clear and sure.
When all bad thought is banished,
will everything be pure.
Should we look for a portal to pass through,
into another age.
Or do we live in a giant book,
and live life page by page.

Is there a path to Enlightenment,
has anyone ever found it?
Lives are spent to search in vain,
but still they try, again and again.
Many men have looked for it,
for over a thousand years.

Never finding an answer, only many tears.
The human brain has many locked doors,
the secret is finding the key.
Is this the way to Enlightenment,
will we finally, see.

Dreams

As we sit in the morning at breakfast,
eating our porridge and cream.
Our brain has still not awakened,
as we think of last night's dream.
We try to remember the detail,
did our dream make us happy or sad.
Did we win the National Lottery,
think hard, its driving us mad.
We try to remember the numbers,
we dream of riches and fame.
But before we know, we're back in bed,
and the cycle commences again.

Cruelty of Man

The mighty Eagle swifty soars,
high above her Eyrie nest.
Watching humans steal an egg,
very soon they'll steal the rest.
She'll have to try again next year,
of that there is no doubt.
She fights a losing battle,
time is running out.
Her fears there are so many,
she'll face them when she can.
Not of global warming,
but the cruelty of man.

Mind Games

When the Odds are stacked against you,
and it seems you can only lose.
Just continue playing your game,
and imagine you've wings on your shoes.

Try and learn to forget the score,
forget that they are one goal more.
Let your thoughts look forward, not behind,
wipe their score out from your mind

Never recognise impending defeat,
heed these words and seldom be beat.
Believe the game has just begun,
when in fact it's nearly done

Keep on believing you play for fun,
Close your eyes and run, run run.
Try and ignore the noise and the din
and at times you will play very badly and win.

Church Mouse

The Bishop thought all eyes were on him,
as he preached on the importance of God's house.
But the eyes of the packed congregation,
were fixed on a playful Mouse.
As the Bishop continued his sermon,
his face so serious and gaunt.
The little mouse had its morning swim,
across the Baptism Font.
The worshippers tittered with laughter,
the Bishop was very perplexed and red.
"Good gracious, what's so funny,
was it something I may have said?"
A little boy ran across the aisle,
and lifted the Mouse by its tail.
A cheer went up, everyone laughed,
would order now prevail.

Work

When the Alarm Clock rings in the morning,
and we try and get out of bed.
We know we must go into work,
or else we'll not be paid.
We need to get those monthly cheques,
to pay our Bills, which come in packs.
But we carry on as usual,
we run the extra mile.
And when we see a happy home,
It makes it all worthwhile.

Earth Warming

We hear of Global warming,
the earth is heating up each day.
We must take steps to cool it down,
there is no other way.
No more burning coal or peat,
no more gas or oil.
The Coral Reefs are dying,
everything on the boil.
Glaciers are on the move,
and as many species go extinct,
we really have a lot to prove.
Heavy rain and flooding,
hot sun and burnt-out grass.
The Bible forecasts Armageddon,
will it come to pass?
Plastic in our Oceans,
no ice for the Polar Bear.
We must all work together,
and show we really care.

Love Nor Money

Mother, mother the young girl said,
why do you think I've never wed.
Is it the wart on the end of my nose
or maybe my hairless head
No no, her mother replied,
to men you'll be sweetness and honey.
As they stand at the end of your bed at night,
counting all of your money.

Day to Day Living

In these times of worry and stress,
when normal living is in such a mess.
As we watch prices rise for Electric and Oil,
and the cost to bring a kettle to boil.
Mother looks at her children and hopes to look cool,
as she tries to fill a lunch box for school.
Father needs money to fill up the car,
the children need new shoes.
The milkman raps the door for money,
this year there'll be no Golf Club dues.
Granny pulls out the candles,
the source of light in days long past.
And Granda he sticks new soles on shoes,
with studs to make them last.
Will things get better we ask with a frown,
prices they always seem to go up,
but rarely ever come down.

Portrush

Blue sky, gentle breeze, clouds like cotton wool.
Seagulls fighting over food,
children playing, free from school.
Families on the beach, playing on the sand,
Surfers needing a helping hand.
Tourist Coaches fill the Park,
lining up from dawn till dark.
As cars arrive, they join a race,
to find themselves a parking space.

Bathers running for a dip, dreaming of a Fish and Chip.
From the Golf Club, shouts of 'Fore'
as players fret about their score.
Soon evening comes, things quieten down,
we don't mind a shower of rain.
The town it rests and sleeps,
before we start it all again.
Nothing ever in a rush,
a Summer's Day in wonderful PORTRUSH.

The Train

Is the name of the engine Thomas,
said the boy as they boarded the train.
I've no idea, replied his mother,
just glad to get out of the rain.
Will it go fast, or will it go slow,
it's so exciting, I'd love to know.
I've no idea, she replied,
just be quiet and enjoy the ride.
Will it stop at all the stations,
will we hear it toot its whistle.
Does it stop at Lanark town,
or go on to Partick Thistle.
Just be quiet his mother said,
as she closed her eyes for a slumber,
Count all the cows you see in the fields,
and tonight you can tell me the number.

The Final Call

When Father Time comes calling,
and we listen for his knock.
We would give all we have, and more,
to stop and turn back the clock.
He'll smile and slowly shake his head,
at attempts to flee the scene of our final breath.
and show there is no way at all,
to avoid our coming death.

Will Father Time take us upwards.
Did we live Life well.
Or will our route be downwards,
down to the Gates of Hell.
In life we believe we have problems,
problems from wall to wall.
But in the end they don't matter,
nothing matters at all.

Modern Warfare

What are my Weapons of choice,
Bombs or Bullets, or just my voice.
We're stockpiling Islamophobia.
The suppliers are asking for more.
I think the only answer is,
we need a larger Store.
Bags of Hatred are in demand,
Antisemitic shirts are selling well.
Tins of Racism are up in price,
we're running out of ill-will Gel!
Be radical they teach,
but don't allow free speech.
Except of course it suits your side,
if not, I'm afraid, its woe betide.

The Dawn Chorus

I heard the sound this morning,
and almost shed a tear.
The noise was so uplifting,
the first Dawn Chorus of the year.

Just for a second, I forgot all the woes,
of the lives we live today,
And for a little time at least,
I felt my troubles drain away.

The concert venue is Sligo Park,
with beautiful trees and greenery.
And when the Larks are first to sing,
it adds magic to the scenery.

The Blue Tit dips and dances,
his tail is very long.
A very solitary bird,
he sings a lovely song.

The Magpies try to do their best,
but melodies they lose.
A very superstitious bird,
it's better when they come in twos.

The Robin and the Wren,
puff their chests and sing,
completely unaware of the pleasure that they bring,
a daily competition to see who is the king.

The Song Thrush and the Blackbird,
sing solo in the Choir.
I felt a tingle down my neck,
no-one can sing any higher.

The conductor is the Black Crow,
as he can only squawk.
But if you listen carefully,
you'll hear that he can almost talk.

The Eagle soars high in the sky,
an unrepentant sinner.
He views the members of the chorus,
thinking of his dinner.

Listening to these magical notes,
fills me full of glee,
and it's really, really, wonderful,
that the concert is all for free.

A Penny For Your Thoughts

Do we feel like applause, or breaking into song,
as our Brain hosts little dreams all day long.
Unconscious thought and Daydreams,
each play out their course,
separating fact from fiction,
from whatever source.
At times we are down in doubtful mood,
things are not happening as they should.
Our thoughts are non-stop all day long,
are we right or are we wrong.

At night our thoughts, they turn to Dreams.
Dreams with no control.
Causing havoc with our Brain,
and tugging at our Soul.
Is there a price on thoughts we ask,
of which we have so many.
There is of course, but we'll not grow rich,
as we are never offered more than a penny.

Cereal

On Monday it's Cornflakes,
on Tuesday its Bran.
On Wednesday it's Porridge,
eat it if you can.
On Thursday we eat Muesli,
on Friday Coco Pops,
eaten on their own,
they really are the tops.
On Saturday it's Weetabix,
on Sunday just a spoon of Honey,
as by the time, we reach this day,
we're surely out of money.

Children

Some children start life so happy,
and some have a start that is sad.
Many will lead a normal life,
And others, of course, will be bad.

Many will want to do well at school,
But others they couldn't care less.
Is this the fault of the parents,
the answer is anyone's guess.

They will follow separate colours,
and all will go their own way,
Each will have a different goal,
and play for it come what may.

Some children wear a smile,
and some they wear a frown.
Many will head to Foreign Lands,
and others will never leave town.

Many will face Adversity,
and lead lives of trouble and strife.
Many will age and live on their own,
others will find a husband or wife.

Some will go on to successful careers,
others may never even try.
But the child who will prosper the furthest in life,
is the one who always asks why.

Awareness

Why should we feel vexed,
when oft' the problem is our own.
We fail to see what others see,
the troubles we have surely sown.
So cast a care for friend and foe,
and listen to their tales of woe.
The key to Love is easily found,
and there for all who look around.
So, hasten help a Soul to-day,
and make their troubles go away.

Marriage

How do you know you're in love.
How do you know it's time to marry.
Is she the one to share your life,
is he the one your dreams to carry?
How do we know when to take the leap,
and make those vows we have to keep.
Does it hurt when she leaves at the end of the day.
Do you think you'll love him come what way.
Just try very hard with all your might,
and hope your dreams will turn out right.
And as we skip through life's long dance,
Everything in the end is down to chance.
Just bear in mind we all have a date,
with the ever-present Mr. Fate.

The Model

As she strode down the catwalk,
she felt a loud tear.
Everyone laughed, something was bare.
Unperturbed she continued her stride,
knowing she was showing her bare Backside.
She didn't look down on her Modelling Gown,
but held her head up high,
As she felt the draught, and everyone laughed,
she could only smile and sigh.
The crowd they clapped and whistled,
her face it bore a grin.
She didn't flinch at her problems,
but took it on the chin.
The moral of this story is,
if your Knickers ever tear,
put a smile upon your face,
and show you don't really care.

Signs of Age

Slower rising from the chair,
watching quickly greying hair.
Walking gently, not so quick,
use a helpful Walking Stick.

Tablets in the morning,
tablets late at night.
Watching our Cholesterol,
keeping everything right.

Someone else to cut the lawn,
always feeling slightly cold.
Electric blanket in the bed,
all the signs of growing old.

Slower getting out of cars,
slower getting into bed.
Turning up the TV volume,
buying papers, never read.

Spectacles, and memory loss,
no more using Dental Floss.
No more late nights out in town,
days spent in your Dressing Gown.

Signs of Age - cont.

No more running,
harder walking up a hill.
Using old age Bus Pass,
no more Petrol Tanks to fill.

Colours growing dim,
False Teeth in a glass.
Everything seems so unforgiving,
Very soon there'll be no more living.

Nightmares

Some Dreams are warm and happy,
we are Actors in a play.
Mostly they take place at night-time,
but sometimes during the day.
These are known as Daydreams,
of which we may have many.
Sometimes we dream of happy times,
spoil them if you dare.
but when we dream of bad things,
a Nightmare crawls out from his Lair.
We do not want good Dreams to end,
we want such Dreams to last.
We wish to wake up with a smile,
and hope the Nightmare Dream has passed.

Let Not a Teardrop Fall

Let the Black Horse clop his shoe on the road,
as the Final Bell is rung.
Let the mourners take their hats off,
and the Psalms and the Hymns be sung.

Have not the people bow their heads,
let not a Teardrop fall.
The life he lived was straight and true,
he spread his love to all.

When Primal fear shall come to nought,
and Earths disorders cease.
The Soul shall rise in wonderful bloom,
and gain immortal peace.

Christmas Dinner

Christmas has passed we've eaten our dinner,
very few of us look any thinner.
But a little piglet whose name was Sammy,
wondered why we ate his Mammy.

Am I also, destined to be a Ham,
is that why my name is Sam.
The Turkey and the Goose have an annual fear,
that they'll end up on our plates each year.

"It's just not fair" cried the Turkey to the Duck,
that at Christmas every year, we have such luck.
No-one cares of the animal's plight,
we're destined to be a 'bloody' sight.

Christmas is a happy time,
it really must be said,
but why do so many Animals,
have to end up dead.

The Theatre of Dreams

The early sunlight dances through the Windowpane,
it brings another day again.
As the darkness leaves, the Playhouse closes it door.
It's been a long eventful night,
do I want the play to end,
or do I want some more.
I see my friends and family,
long gone this life for many years,
I see their faces, feel their tears.
I lie and think, and think,
and then I think again.
Am I really in a Playhouse,
watching scenes from life gone by,
everyone seems to be living,
did they really die?
The short winter day soon passes,
darkness clouds the Windowpane.
I really must try and get some sleep,
before the Playhouse Curtains rise again.

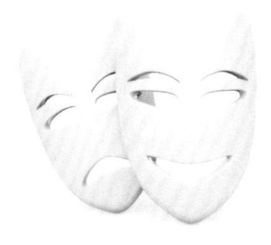

The Passing Wind

The smell it came with the sound,
there was nowhere it could drift.
Everyone tried to hold their breath,
they were going up in a Lift.

They looked around at each other,
seeking someone to blame.
The second was more a puff than a noise,
but the smell was just the same.

"First floor", said the Operator,
smiling and feeling hearty.
The only one who knew,
that he was the guilty party.

Lonely Ben

Ben Bulben holds his lonely sway,
lording over Sligo Bay.
Looking down on Cliffony and Grange,
Last remnant of a mountain range.
Forever staring at his Queen,
who also views the wonderous scene.
His cry of loneliness can be heard,
when sounds they fade at night.
Maeve, Queen Maeve, hold my hand,
hold it 'till morning light.
Mighty Ben Bulben, she cries from her cairn,
atop of Knocknaree,
I will hold your hand, for all Eternity.
Maeve, oh Maeve, I hear your cry,
you are never from my sight.
You feel my pain, you really know my plight.
My tears are the Garvogue River,
it carries them out to sea.
Someday we'll move together
whenever that may be.
I'll hold your hand in mine, and sing,
before the end of everything.

Sweet Life

I love Custard and Jelly,
I've loved it all my life.
I'd swap anything for a helping,
I'd even swap my wife.

"Is that the case, his wife replied,
you like the finer things in life.
But if you don't change your outlook,
I'll no longer be your wife!"

"I was wrong to say such an awful thing,
I'm really very contrite.
For that I'll buy you a diamond ring,
will everything be alright.

"That will be fine,
thanks for the ring,
no more if and but.
I think you've learned your lesson,
Just keep your big mouth shut."

The Purpose of Life

What is the purpose of life,
is this for you to decide?
You can think one way or another,
and hope you enjoy the ride.
Try not to let emotions fly,
when daily tasks are causing a sigh.
Always be kind to others,
Compassion is a noble state.
Always act with love, never showing hate.
Some spend their lifetime wisely,
some don't really care.
Some will raise a family,
others wouldn't dare.
Does anyone know of their Granny's Granny,
except in a photo on a wall.
It's as if they never existed, never existed at all.
The fruits of life we eat in haste,
will surely suffer loss of taste.
So just when you think your problems are great,
your worst lies ahead, his name is Fate.
Tis best to live life day by day,
there really is no other way.
Try not to worry, take things in your stride,
when Mr. Fate comes calling,
you'll find there is no place to hide.

Good or Bad

The young can stray in early years,
and chase some doubtful Themes.
Hopes are, that in the prime of Life,
they realise some righteous dreams.
Are innocent children all born good,
is bad and evil cloaked with a hood.
The young whose path is straight and narrow,
in Adulthood have much less sorrow.
Do we teach our children,
as often as we should.
To recognise right from wrong,
To recognise bad from good.
To recognise a falling Star,
bringing evil from afar.
Teach them Grace,
to be kind in every way,
and they'll be happy,
till their dying day.

Happiness

Where are you going Granddaughter, he asked,
why are you dressed in your very best coat?
I'm going to search for Happiness Granda,
I'm sailing off on the very next boat.

No, no her Granda replied,
that's not what you do,
You never search for Happiness,
Happiness comes to you.

How will I know when it reaches me,
I really can't wait very long.
You will know her Granda replied,
you'll return and sing me a song.

She closed her eyes and wished,
and then she wished again.
She had to find her Happiness,
and she had to know just when.

She travelled and she searched,
she went from door to door.
From high up in the mountains,
down to the sandy shore.

She finally found the answer,
and learned what Happiness was.
A wonderful, beautiful state of mind,
a sunbeam in our earthly cause.

I've found it Granda, I've found it,
can you see how happy I am.
Everything is warm and cosy,
I'm in a wonderland.

Well done Granddaughter, well done,
you didn't need to burst into song.
It's great you found your Happiness.
It was here with you all along.

Granny's Whistle

The children pricked their ears,
the sound they understood.
The noise was Granny's whistle,
calling them for food.
They ran down from the Sandhills,
making it a race.
Who would be first to the caravan,
and Granny's smiling face.
The years roll by and memories are made,
and those of our wonderful Granny,
will never ever fade.

Experience

A time to listen, a time to speak.
A time to turn the other cheek.
To know just when is the secret,
not solved by swallowing a pill.
Experience is a lengthy state of mind,
it cannot be bought at will.
A penny for your thoughts,
is a question we often hear,
'Tis better to ignore this,
to answer might cost us dear.
Gain prudence with age,
said the wise old sage.
Read the facts very carefully,
before you turn the page.
When things start to look unimportant,
and we lay our secrets bare.
We will surely realise,
we've grown too old to care.

Return of Summer

The earthy smell of fresh cut grass,
the heavy Rose it dances on its slender stem.
The buzz of many Honeybees,
is Summer really back again?
Children laughing noisily,
at last they're free from school.
They plead to Mum and Dad,
please take us to the Swimming pool.
Dad seeks out his gardening tools,
lots to do before the rain.
Discard the heavy trousers, put on the Shorts,
is Summer really back again?
Going to bed in daylight, as the day is now very long.
The Cock he crows in the morning,
He thinks he's singing a song.
Shall we go to the beach for a picnic, says mum,
and hope it doesn't rain.
Is Summer really back again?
The cows they leave the cowshed,
happy to be back in the meadow.
The birds they sing in the morning,
in sunshine and in rain,
Their song is good to the ear,
is Summer really back again?

Hell's Gate

The Gates of Hell they never close,
the road well-lit with a path that glows.
The Devil he has many wiles,
to start us on this track.
And once we start the journey,
it's difficult turning back.
Thus as down the stream of life we sail,
what grand delusions oft o'er sense prevail.
We tend to imagine each coming scene
and wish that grass was always green.
When Rainbows form, enchanting to the view,
they evade our grasp and flee as we pursue.
Keep an eye out for temptation,
lead a life that's true come what may.
Avoiding all the subtle signs,
that lead the other way.

The Proposal

Let's get wed the Gentleman said,
I can half your trouble.
"Nay, nay" she replied, shaking her head,
my trouble would surely double.
Not so Madame he replied,
we can share our cost.
"No sir, no sir" she replied, my virtue would be lost.
Your virtue is quite safe, he said,
I'll not share your bed.
All I need is company,
and a stomach kept well fed.

Love

Love does not drop so easily,
at times it needs a prod.
And when it seems its lost forever,
we place our hope in God.

The secret to a happy life,
on our limited time on this earth.
Is to find someone to love and share it with,
and live in peace and mirth.

We pray the evil flames of strife,
shall not appear to us in life.
Once you find love, hold it tight,
through the day and through the night.

Pity those who lose it,
pity those who fail to find,
And when you have a wonderful love,
never let it leave your mind.

Destroy it at your peril,
if you ever dare.
True Love never runs smoothly,
when it does it's very rare.

Hope Springs

The Camelia and Daffodil show when its spring,
has the winter gone away.
Can we pull out our Sandals, shake off the dust,
as we feel the brighter, warmer day.
As the temperature rises, so do our hopes,
of a better year than before.
Will we be happy with what we have,
or will we always look for more.

Politics

Political Parties they come and go,
Lib, Dem, Labour or Tory.
They huff and they puff as they plod along,
but peddle the same old story.
They each draft a Manifesto,
and promise with all their might,
but once in power, "Hey presto"
they seldom put anything right.

The Blackbird

Some mornings I awaken,
to a really magical trill.
The song of a Blackbird,
near my bedroom Windowsill.
He warbles and whistles,
and calls for a date,
I hope it succeeds,
in attracting a mate.
To hear this bird sing his morning song,
is to banish worry and trouble.
It's a wonderful way to start the day,
our enthusiasm for life is double.

Life and Death

Two often used words,
are Life and Death.
Of one you speak loudly,
the other under your breath.
The first is given by your Mother,
the second you learn as you grow.
One always leads to the other,
there is no other way to go.

Precious Moments

One of the wonderful moments in life,
which happens time after time.
Is the wide-eyed innocence of a child,
listening to a Nursery Rhyme

But soon the innocence will fade,
as time it hurries past.
Time it changes everything,
alas, the die is cast.

For the pureness of these moments,
parents should shed some tears.
These are precious memories,
to carry down life's years.

Living

Knowledge is the answer,
but keep an open mind.
Listen to another view,
a view of a different kind.
What outcome from this union of thought,
for all who listen, and want to be taught.
Can it be the seed of hope,
will we ever learn to cope?
As our Planet spins between her Poles,
face down Adversity, and achieve your goals.
We each have a different course to run,
and a different flag to follow in life.
The word we must learn is compassion,
avoiding trouble and strife.

Dubai

Dubai, Dubai, warm and sunny,
Camels and Sand,
blue skies and money.
Sheiks and Ferrari's,
sunshine on the boil,
no Income Tax or VAT,
just revenue from oil.
Wearing straw made Sandals,
no need for any laces.
Living in large tents,
enjoying Camel Races.
Where men wear white dresses,
have black beards and covered heads,
have afternoon siestas lying in their beds.
This quickly growing Country,
this land of milk and honey.
New rows of buildings in the sand,
people obsessed with money.
But if the sun were to vanish, with permanent rain,
would we visit Dubai again?

A Promise

What is this thing,
that one can give.
More valuable than Gold,
or the right to live.
It's never to break a promise,
and always keep your word.
Keep these rules in life,
and you'll always be heard.
Even a promise we only imply,
must always be true, and never a lie.

Late Autumn

The warmth has gone,
the temperature is growing cold,
the clock has gone back, we're told.
Leaves falling off the trees,
brought down by a gentle breeze.

The noise of water as it flows,
gently down a stream.
The grass is covered by a dew,
the air is crisp and clean.

Noisy Crows break the silence,
fighting for a worm or two.
Turtle Doves they watch the scene,
calling out, coo, coo, coo coo.
The Frogs they make a laboured croak,
hidden by the leafy cloak.

A cheeky Robin tries to steal,
a portion of a Squirrel's nut.
Keeping an eye on a Forester,
sitting by his Hut.

Children standing at the bus stop,
just returned to School,
wearing their new Overcoats,
their scarves are made of wool.

The Hedges some days white with frost,
no more flowers to see.
Snow is not too far away,
silence from the Honey Bee.

Feeling sad that Summer has passed,
Winter is very near.
Another year has passed us by,
you are allowed to shed a tear.

The Bus Pass

I've had my old age Bus Pass,
for twenty years and more.
Does this mean I am really old,
older than four score?
"You're as old as you feel,
and you're very good at that as one can see,'
said the lady as she climbed down from his knee.

The Mobile Phone

My Mobile Phone can do anything,
it can even pay my Bills.
It can take me a drive on the Internet,
it can even order my Pills.
I can watch a Movie or talk to a friend,
read a Book, or a message send.
I can book a flight on a Plane,
take photos of all I survey.
Or play an Internet game,
at night or during the day.
I remember the days of the Call Box,
when a call was only four pence.
I can now use my phone to Bank,
it's very hard to make sense.

Lucky

To be lucky in Love,
is the greatest gift of all.
Hold it tight in your heart,
never let it fall.

Think hard and reason why,
if you ever make her sad, or cry.
Be honour bound, and keep your vow,
to love and cherish, 'till you die.

Look at her sleeping beside you,
think how fortunate you are in life.
and as you lie and watch her sleep,
be very glad you made her your Wife.

In daytime her smile is continuous,
she looks in the eye as she speaks.
She has given you the greatest gift of all,
little children with rosy cheeks.

Choice

As we take part in life's long dance,
we learn that outcomes are down to chance.
Odds or Evens, red or blue,
boy or a girl, it's never up to you.
What decides the outcome,
of the toss of a coin or a dice,
brown eyes or blue,
either look very nice.
We make many choices daily,
that's how life is run.
You make one choice or the other,
just make sure, you make the right one.

Broadhaven Bay

Please take me home to Ireland,
take me come what may.
I've finished all my wandering,
and I fear I've lost my way.

Please take me home to Ireland,
I dream of her every day.
Back to beautiful Mayo,
Belmullet and Broadhaven Bay.

War Memories

It was the Spring of 1941,
I started School that year.
The Bombs were falling in Belfast,
the pupils hadn't much to cheer.

No playing in the Playground,
when the Sirens made their wailing sounds.
Hiding under our Desks,
everything else was out of bounds.

We had to flee up the mountain,
up to the Horseshoe bend.
The children were fearful and worried,
was the World about to end.

We listened to the all clear Siren,
the bombing raid was over at last.
Everyone breathed a sigh of relief,
the danger seemed to have passed.

No more worries about spelling,
or counting up to five.
The main aim in a Pupils life
was trying to stay alive.

There were no Guidance Counsellors,
'Mental Health' hadn't come into play.
Children just got on with life,
and lived from day to day.

War

How do we define a War,
what does the word really mean.
Has one side annoyed the other,
so badly it can't be fixed,
Has one side annoyed the other,
their blood can never be mixed.
If words, or a stroke of pen,
are not enough to save the day.
Must we take the letting of blood
to be the only other way.
All Wars eventually finish,
most are settled by elapsing time.
On hindsight it all seems so petty and wrong,
as off-spring wonder why it started,
and why it continued so long.

The Weather

What subject do we mention most,
when we waken each morning,
to our Coffee and Toast.
Is it Money, or is it Love,
or maybe both together.
Not either I'm afraid,
it's all about the Weather.
Something we can never control,
the rain it seeps through heart and soul.
We must accept what comes our way,
smile and hope for a better day,
and hope these dark clouds fade away.
Keep looking for a Rainbow,
they say it stops the rain.
But you can be sure of one thing,
the weather will always change again.

Belief

The Fisherman catches Fish,
the Farmer grows the Crops.
The Engineer makes the Motor Car.
The Weaver takes the wool from the Sheep,
to make the clothing we need to keep warm.
These men are all God fearing,
that is the common thread.
And most will say their prayers to God,
before they go to bed.
But where is this God, who controls our lives,
and invites us to his Paradise.
Should we pray for other people,
whose life is worse than our own.
Why should we pray for enemies,
I hear some people moan.
Is prayer the last resort,
when everything else has failed.
Is prayer your last throw of the Dice,
when the boat has already sailed.
They teach us of a God in Heaven,
and that he can hear our prayer.
Or maybe we need to see a Miracle,
to prove that he's up there.
Or do we gather and lend our voice,
have the belief, and really rejoice.

Chance

Mighty Eros, God of Love,
spends his working day,
sprinkling Stardust from above,
making people fall in love,
has he the final say?
Eros may guide, but I will decide,
and when he waves his Magic Wand,
I'll test him with my heavy hand.
Everyone needs to pass my way,
on each and every day or date.
Many hate to say my name,
I'm always there, my name is Fate.
So have a care young lovers
be happy when you dance,
and be aware that life dictates,
that everything is down to chance.

Life

Be aware of how Life flies,
as like a Flower, it seeds,
it buds and blooms,
and then it slowly dies.

Ignorance

The precept is as follows,
that Ignorance is Bliss,
or would you rather know?
Would you rather worry,
and watch your trouble grow?
If we could see ourselves,
as others surely might.
Would we ever change,
would we ever put things right?
Life and Fate are brothers,
of that you can be sure,
intertwined bedfellows,
ever to endure.

Secrets

(PLEASE DON'T SAY TO ANYONE)

Only two people can keep a Secret,
and one of them must be dead,
and the more you request some secrecy,
the more the story will spread.
So, if you don't wish people to know,
keep your Mouth closed, and rumour can't grow.

School Days

In the wee small hours, as the Pussy Cat tires,
of chasing Mice and Flies, and Moths that dance
and flutter in the light.
The sound is only broken by the Milkman in his van,
setting down the Bottles as quietly as he can.
A dog barks in the distance, two cats appear to fight,
the Dawn breaks slowly from the East
it's the ending of the night.

Tired eyes they start to see, awakened from their slumbers,
the smell of Bacon on the pan, and Coffee cups in numbers.
The rustle sound of Cornflakes, Yogurt by the dish,
burning Toast and Marmalade, the smell of Mackerel fish.
I've lost my Tie, a child will cry,
but Mother says, don't make a fuss.
Find it if you can, but please don't miss the Bus.

In Winter Time the ground is hard,
it's walking Boots on ice,
innocent faces stare at books,
purchased at a dreadful price.
The children pile into Dad's new car,
and think of homework not done, exams to come,
and tend to view their troubles from afar.

Then they are gone, and Mum sits down,
she relaxes with a sigh,
she is left all alone with her Mobile Phone,
and a list of things to buy,
for an Evening meal, for Lunch at school,
and her husband's morning Fry.
After School, it's home to Mum and the smell
of cooking food.
This changes all the attitudes,
and makes them all feel good.

It's very soon dark, and they head for bed,
and listen to the rain.
The door is opened, and out runs the cat,
to start the whole thing off again.
Is this we ask a normal day, is every house the same?
If the answer is YES feel happy,
it's only part of Life's long game.

Life and Strife

When War and trouble far away
affects us in our working day,
by driving up the price of Oil, and Gas, and food.
We try to lead a normal life,
and lift our sombre mood,
and as we learn our further strife,
that complicates our day,
what price this life, you may very easily say.
As we watch the ever-rising cost of living,
and daily tasks seem unforgiving,
let us think of those worse off than we,
whose pain and misery is there for all to see.
Help them now, let us not defer,
with love and care, and help to make them bear,
the life they live from day to day,
and make their troubles go away.

Hands-free Doctors

The Doctors sat drinking their Coffee,
their eyes very soon grew wide.
A Patient was at the surgery door,
there was no place to hide.

We'll have to let them in, said one,
and listen to their trouble.
Not so, not so, another cried,
if we see them, our trouble will double!

If we see this Patient, word will spread,
And more will arrive, they are easily lead.
Keep them on the phone, never face to face,
No one-to-one consultation whatever the case.

Patients will have to stop being ill,
it causes the Doctors much tension.
They would like a Patient-free life,
as they gallop towards their Pension.

Bags of Happiness and Laughter

Pray what do you sell in this Shop, he said,
    as he strode in through the door.
Why we sell Laughter and Happiness sir,
    we're full from ceiling to floor.
But the shop looks empty to me, he said,
    there's nothing on the shelves.
Oh yes there is, can you not see we're full,
    of Children, laughing amongst themselves.
I can hear nothing I still think it's bare
    I still believe there's nothing there.
"Try hard, try hard" said the member of Staff
    and you will hear the Children laugh.
Just close your eyes and make a wish,
    for a dip into the Happiness dish.
Wish for Happiness and Laughter all round,
    and only then will you hear the sound.
I will, I will, he cried, and closed his eyes to fears,
and he heard the sound of the Laughter ringing in his ears.
I'll take a bag of Happiness, he cried, amongst his tears.
    I'll give you some money, I'll pay you a fee,
He replied "You owe me nothing, everything's free!"

Absence

As we journey away from our loved ones,
by accident or design.
Such absence really hurts a lot,
and prays upon the mind.
But think of all the things good in life,
forget about the absence pain
Think of all the Happiness stored,
until we meet again.

Wishes

To hold your Baby in your arms.
To pass a School Exam.
To kiss a Mother just once more,
we hadn't time to say goodbye.
To win the National Lottery.
To flap your arms and fly.
To change my baldness for a little hair.
To be lucky in the spouse we choose,
many win, but many loose.
To have three more wishes,
or would that be unfair.
To suffer no more pain.
To change things back the way they were.
That my horse will win,
and make me very wealthy.
To never have an Illness,
staying very healthy.
For funds to buy the Children's shoes,
and a little more to pay our Dues.
I wish your wishes all come true,
and make the World a happier place,
for you, and you, and you.

What Others See

Wouldn't you love to see what others see in us,
wouldn't you love to hear their whispers.
Wouldn't you like to catch their wink,
or is it maybe better, that we don't know what they think.
We hear of keeping to the straight and narrow,
never accuse and never borrow.
Try to understand things fully,
the reason for the Classroom Bully.
Pity him, he'll never win,
no matter what his awful sin.
Hope to see the good in Men,
and hope that they see such in us.
Live and love in honesty,
and never make a fuss.
Slow the pace of the life you know,
when your time is up, you'll have to go.

The Robin

A flash of red on the Windowsill,
he taps the glass with his Shiny Bill.
His song is sharp and breaks the air,
he's looking for some breakfast fare.
    The little sparrows fly away,
        the Robin is the boss.
    He receives his Breakfast,
        the others pick at Moss.

Early Winter

The copper colour of Autumn,
appears amongst the trees.
A quieter chorus at the dawn,
no more Bumble Bees.
The Squirrels, they have buried their nuts,
the days are growing colder.
No more leaves to blow in the wind,
the Stags are growing bolder.
Summer is a memory,
the Lark has stopped it's morning song.
We'll soon have frost and snow
and Winter before very long.

The Unspoken Word

Please kind sir, what are you thinking,
I'd love to know what's on your mind.
Will you tell me the truth,
or are you the lying kind.

No sir, I'm not the lying kind,
but I may not say what's on my mind.
Many thoughts must remain hidden,
to diverge is surely forbidden.

Many times we promise not to say,
we must not break this trust.
We give this promise every day,
and keep it, we surely must.

Many times we nod or shake our head,
the mouth remains firmly shut.
It's easier to fix what's not been said,
avoiding an IF or a BUT.

Hope

Hope and Aspiration is with us when we're small.
Hope and Aspiration is open for us all.
The young they dream of what will lie ahead,
of a life all good, and plans well laid.
Some may laugh, and others cry,
as hopes are shattered and slowly die.
Life is full of crossroads,
with signs that often lie.
Sometimes fate will lend a helping hand,
and maybe guide us to a Promised Land.
Many will fear and shed a tear,
where o' where did they make their mistake,
as they watch their hopes fade and break.
Some will surely reach that better place,
living a life of Honesty and Grace.
Work hard, work hard, will all your might,
and maybe, just maybe, things will be alright.

The Rush

No let up for the Human Race,
we live our lives at such a pace.
We try to be first, never last,
everything seems to be rushing past.
We rush and bustle through our day,
as if there is no other way.
Have we got what it takes, to apply the brakes,
can we slow down, and smell the honey,
and forget about winning and money.
Our days will soon be over,
of that there is no doubt,
and at the end we'll realise,
just what Life was all about.

Innocence

Children are all born innocent,
and enter such a cruel world to-day.
Some are born out of love,
and others another way.
Many from mistakes,
and some out of trouble and strife.
What price their future?
What price, they'll lead a normal life.
We look at a sea of faces,
it's the first day of Nursery School.
All looking prim and proper,
their teacher trying to look cool.
Some children play with toys,
some they play in the pit of sand.
Some they draw with crayons,
some smile and clap their hands.
But the loudest clap of all,
and the one with the biggest smile,
was the little girl born from brutality.
Her clap was the loudest,
and her smile was the best by a mile.
All children are allowed equal dreams,
as nothing in life is ever as it seems.

The Huntsman

Stillness, Silence,
the light is fading fast.
At the Forest edge, some Deer appear,
they do not break the quiet here,
but stand like statues,
the only movement is their ears.
As they listen for any danger,
the Huntsman lowers his rifle,
taken by the scene.
He will not break the silence to-night.

No

Marry me, Marry me, I promise I'll change my ways,
I'll work very hard from morning till night,
until my dying days.
The answer is 'no', you've asked before,
but you haven't changed your ways in life.
Not only do you drink too much,
you are always looking for more.
Please give me another chance, said the man,
for you I'll stop my drinking.
The answer is 'NO', replied the lady,
I'll never change my mind.
You may be very good looking,
but you are not the marrying kind.

The Red Squirrel

Pray tell me Red Squirrel, what will you do,
what will you do to-day?
I'll climb some Trees, watch out for the Bees,
and laugh as the branches sway.
Then I'll come down and dig up some nuts,
that I buried in summer last year.
Then I'll chase away the noisy Crows,
the din really hurts my ear.
Then I'll dance in the wind, with the Butterflies,
and watch the children below.
And as they wave, I'll be very brave,
and I'll try to put on a good show.

Gift or Talent

Some people have a fire that fiercely burns,
it's always there, and twists and turns.
It may be love, it may be Talent,
or maybe a gift unknown.
The problem is to know it's there, and to use it.
Never let it slip and try and never lose it.
Think of what others would give for your gift,
think of the pain they'd endure.
It's a sin to squander a Talent or Gift,
of that you can be sure.
A limited time is set on Gifts, you must use it with all your will,
as every night that passes, every night that goes by,
the flame will grow dimmer still.
So grab it now, grasp it with both hands to-day,
show the World your talent, banish fear away.
Use your Gift, and lead a Life that's clean,
pray the day is far away, when your Talent is no longer seen.

Scotia

Scotia, O' mighty Scotia,
Father of Erin's Isle, and Tongue.
Now lost in time, and whose name is never sung.
Untruths they never take a rest,
and try to cling to History's Breast.
Please forgive those who would deny,
and in ignorance, believe a Lie.
The truth may not be altered, nor any fact or date.
To do so would be wrongful,
and lead to tempting Fate.

Copy of page 62 and 63 "A Child's History of Ireland" by P.W. Joyce, LLD, Ireland's foremost Ancient Historian, author of 13 books on Irish history and language. This shows the reason for the poem Scotia. Until Independence, his books were widely used in school curriculums.

'Those who have read the early history of England will remember that the Picts and Scots, marching southwards from the Scottish Highlands, gave much trouble, year after year for a long period, to the Romans and Britons. The Picts were the people of Scotland at the time; and the Scots were the Irish, who crossing over to Alban or Scotland, joined the Picts in their formidable raid's southwards. We know all this, not only from our own native Historians, but also from Roman writers, who tell us how the Romans had often to fight in Britain against the Scots from Ireland. For at that time Ireland was called (among other names) Scotia; and the Irish people were known as Scots. When, subsequently, the Irish made settlements and founded a kingdom in Scotland. Ireland was usually called Scotland, while Scotland, whose old name was Alban, became known as "Scotia Minor". This continued to the eleventh or twelfth century, when our own country dropped the name Scotia and was called Eire-land then Ireland, from the old native name Eire or Erin; and Alban came to be known by its present name Scotland, that is, the land of the Scots or Irish. The language in Ireland at that time, up to the 11th century was Scots Gallic'.

The Wrong Man

She awoke the first morning,
of her new wedded life.
Her ears were sore,
at her Husband's snore,
was she now really his wife?
Through her tousled hair, the tears they ran,
as she suddenly knew, she had wed the wrong man.
So, think twice before you marry,
make sure you love and care.
This will save sleepless nights,
and prevent a life of despair.

The Grim Reaper

Grim Reaper, Grim Reaper,
who ends life's long race.
Can you pray tell me,
the time, and the place?
I only determine the time and the day,
the place you will be, is for you to say.

Grim Reaper, Grim Reaper,
may I ask of you,
will your visit be expected,
or out of the blue?
The rules determine, I may not reply,
I must not tell you when you'll die.

Where will I go when you end it all,
will it be heaven or hell.
I cannot tell where your soul will go,
I only toll the final bell.

Grim Reaper, Grim Reaper,
I hear what you say.
You say you will not name the day.
I can only hope, when you appear,
I'm not at home, you've come the wrong year.

The Lady on the Beach

I walked along the beach one day,
as Dawn broke into the Sky.
The waves were quiet, just a gentle lap,
the silence broken by a seagull's cry.
I spied a Lonely Figure walking towards me on the sand
and as it grew closer, I could see,
a dark clothed Lady wave her hand.
"Don't live your life in anger,
always listen to another view.
Try and be kind to others,
those less fortunate than you."
Then she was gone, vanished there and then,
had I been dreaming, did I really see her,
would she ever appear again?
I looked at where she had stood,
and saw a sparkle in the sand.
I bent and lifted a Golden Ring,
had it fallen from her hand?
I take my daily walk each day,
and watch for her in the wind and rain,
but she never appears, not a glimpse,
will I ever see her again?

The Bishop's Dream

The Piper played the long Lament,
tears were freely shed.
When suddenly the Corpse sat up,
he wasn't really dead.

Some of the mourners fainted
some they let out a cry.
Were they really seeing a Ghost,
did he really die?

The Bishop seemed perturbed,
he hadn't seen anything wrong.
Why were the Mourners fainting,
had his Sermon gone on too long?

He awakened in a sweat,
what did it all really mean?
He felt so happy and relieved,
to discover it was really a dream.

Word Play

Little words they swim around,
deep within the Brain.
They call for Pen and Paper,
and want the hand to write again.

Some days the urge is very great,
and words are forming up too fast.
They want put down on paper,
before their moment in time as passed.

These words they form a Sentence,
in turn they form a Verse.
Each one has a part to play,
before they shall disperse.

Borrowing

Sometimes we do a favour,
to those who will let us down in the end.
Do we grin and bear it,
or never again do we lend.
Tis better to make the loan a gift,
and avoid any future friendship rift.

Rock of Cashel

Wonderful, beautiful, Rock of Cashel, Guardian of Cashel Town,
ancient seat of Munster's Dalcassian Kings, Mahon and Brian,
who helped to rid the Country of the Danish Lion.
Where Myth and Legend remain conjoined,
and unseen forces stay aligned.
Where Ghostly Spirits meet at night,
in the nearby Hore Abbey ruins.
Both Buildings whisper to each other,
barely making any sound.
A nightly peace descends,
and only Souls may wander around.
History and Mystery, bedfellows of an Ancient Past,
make certain Cashel Palace will surely ever last.

This poem is dedicated to my good friends Tom & Brid.

Sand Erosion at Strandhill

Queen Maeve sits proud atop of Knocknaree,
ever watching out to sea.
She looks at life beneath her Throne,
amid the passing years,
where man is quickly making change,
realising her many fears.
Changes to Truth, and Hope and Reason,
the Wheels of Time they grind out, Season after Season.
She watches from her Throne in the skies,
as global temperatures they rise and rise.
She sees the Sandhills at her feet,
erode away where Humans meet.
These hills of sand grown for ten thousand years,
lowered in a thousand days causing many tears.
She notes the changes every day at dawn,
knowing she'll be here when everything else is gone.
Humans they top the Animal Chain,
controlling every Species known.
The Wheels of Time have put them there,
they must account for all they have sown.

Talk

Language is a wonderful part of Life,
to be able to talk to each other,
but it's when the talking stops,
that causes all the bother.

In days gone by we used to debate,
To show all the points of view.
But now our words are used for hate,
And debate only used by a few.

Problems can be solved by talking,
Of that there is no doubt.
All conflicts can be ended,
if we get together and shout.

Future

The World is slowly warming,
it casts an ever-changing face.
As many Species go extinct,
what future for the Human Race.
The Chapel Spire it stands on high,
showing signs of days gone by.
What vision now, what brand of fate,
has our chance to change been left too late.
Do we, in this ever-changing age,
where Mobile Phones are all the rage,
dream of what might be.
Or have we yet to turn the page?

Fate travels fast, no more time to think.
Instant news, instant views, instant judgement in a blink.
Are we born for tears and strife,
or will we lead a blissful life?
When all Disease curls up and disappears,
bringing hope and fewer tears.
Will our imagination take centre stage,
and lead us to a brand-new age?

Our Enemies should now be friends,
no more fighting for whatever ends.
As life unfolds at such a rapid pace,
we must slow down and show some honest grace.
We now make friends with those we've never met,
all arranged by Internet.

Will all this bring us untold Wealth,
or cause us problems with our Mental Health?
Time will tell, it always does,
no matter what our earthly cause.
Or should we trust our daily journey,
the reason for our being,
To one who sits on high, is mighty, and all seeing.

Inspired to write a book?

Contact

Maurice Wylie Media
Your Inspirational & Christian Book Publisher
Based in Northern Ireland, serving readers worldwide

www.MauriceWylieMedia.com